Why should I?

DRINK MORE WATER

Cindy Devine Dalton

The Rourke Book Co, Inc.
Vero Beach, Florida 32964

PHOTO CREDITS
Gibbons Photography

EDITORIAL SERVICES
Pamela Schroeder

Library of Congress Cataloging-in-Publication Data

Dalton, Cindy Devine, 1964-
    Drink more water / Cindy Devine Dalton.
        p. cm. — (Why should I...)
    Includes index.
    ISBN 1-55916-302-X
    1. Water—Physiological effect—Juvenile literature. [1. Water.] I. Title. II. Series

QP535.H1 .D35 2000
613.2'87—dc21
                                          00–028018

Printed in the USA

CONTENTS

DOES YOUR BODY LOOK LIKE WATER?

How much of your body is water? Most of it is! Your body is 65 percent water. Your body is made up of **tissue** and water. The tissue is your bones, muscles and **organs** like your heart and lungs. The water is in your blood, sweat and other body **fluids**.

Your body doesn't look like water, but it is more than half water!

NO WATER, NO LIFE!

You can live for weeks or even months with no food. You can only live for about 10 days with no water. Water is the most important **nutrient**. Our bodies need water to do everything. When our bodies don't get enough water, we are **dehydrated**.

Playing in the hot sun makes your body need to drink more water.

DEHYDRATION WARNING!

Think of your body like a river. If it doesn't rain for a long time, the river will dry up. Your body will do the same. If your body dehydrates, you get sick. You may have a fever and feel sick to your stomach. If you are dehydrated for a long time, your body stops working.

If you become dehydrated you might feel sick or dizzy and have a high temperature.

WATER DOES IT ALL!

Water helps everything in your body work. Water helps you bend your knees and elbows. Water gets rid of wastes in your body. Water carries **oxygen** and nutrients to all parts of your body.

Do you know how your body cools down? It cools down with water. When you sweat the water lies on top of your skin. This cools your skin down and lowers your body's **temperature**.

When you play hard, your body gets rid of the heat by sweating.

Some kids play in the sun and get really hot!

Even if you are trading cards, reading or just lying in the sun, you should drink lots of water.

WATER IS GOOD FOR THE OUTSIDE, TOO!

Water does all kinds of good things for the inside of your body. Water does good things for the outside of your body, too.

If you drink plenty of water, your skin will be soft and smooth. It will not look dry and flaky. Drinking water also helps you have good breath. Water can even help your teeth stay white!

Do you know that celery is more than half water? You can eat a good snack, and help your skin and teeth at the same time.

CUPS AND CUPS EVERY DAY

Your body needs 8 to 10 cups of water every day. If you exercise a lot, or sweat a lot, you need even more. You should drink fluids when you exercise to stop your body from getting too hot.

If you drink enough water, you should urinate about every two hours. **Urination** is our body's way of getting rid of the fluid waste. You should drink enough water to go to the bathroom several times during the day.

You need 8–10 cups of water every day. If you exercise or play a lot, you need even more!

ONLY WATER?

Your body needs fluids. Water is the best fluid for your body because it is pure. However, your body gets water and fluids from other places, too. Your body gets fluid out of the foods you eat. Fruits and vegetables are 80–95 percent water. Meats can be as much as 50 percent, or half, water. Rice and oats are about 35 percent water.

You can get water from many things. Grapefruits, grapes, and strawberries are good choices.

WATER CONTAINS...

Water has no calories. It has no vitamins, fats, or protein. It has no carbohydrates. However, water is the most important thing that you can put into your body. Without water we could not digest our food or get rid of waste. Even though water doesn't seem to have a lot in it, it is very important.

Water and milk are the best choices to drink. They have no sugar or caffeine.

HOW MUCH AND WHEN?

You should drink fluids with every meal and during exercise. Pay close attention to what kind of fluids you drink. Some fluids are good for you. Some are bad. Fluids with **caffeine** are bad. Caffeine can dehydrate your body. Caffeine can make you feel shaky and nervous. Can you think of fluids that are good and do not have caffeine? If you said water, juice, milk, and sports drinks, you did a good job because none of these have caffeine!

GLOSSARY

caffeine (ka FEEN) – substance in foods and liquids that causes a feeling of excitement or nervousness

dehydrated (dee HY drayt) – low amount of fluids in the body

fluids (FLOO idz) – liquids such as milk and water that hydrate the body

nutrient (NOO tree ent) – a substance in foods and liquids that the body uses to function

organs (OR genz) – cells and tissues that combine to do a function

oxygen (AHK se jin) – a gas used by the body

temperature (TEM per ch cher) – the amount of heat or coldness of something

tissue (TISH oo)-a layer of cells that function alike

urination (YUR in NAY shun) – ridding the body of liquid waste

FURTHER READING

Compton's Encyclopedia Online
www.Suite101.com
http.//search.kids.channel.aol.com

INDEX